5.95

D

D1522600

The Story of the Jews

by Julia Neuberger

Illustrated by Chris & Hilary Evans

Cambridge University Press

Cambridge

London   New York   New Rochelle
Melbourne   Sydney

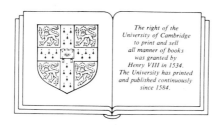

The right of the
University of Cambridge
to print and sell
all manner of books
was granted by
Henry VIII in 1534.
The University has printed
and published continuously
since 1584.

Published by the Press Syndicate of the University of Cambridge
The Pitt Building, Trumpington Street, Cambridge CB2 1TP
32 East 57th Street, New York, NY 10022, USA
10 Stamford Road, Oakleigh, Melbourne 3166, Australila

First published 1986

Printed in Great Britain

ISBN 0 521 30601 9 hard covers
ISBN 0 521 31580 8 paperback

G&E

What is Judaism?

Judaism is the religion of the Jews. Most Jews were born of Jewish parents, so Judaism is largely passed on from one generation to the next. But there are some people who become Jewish by choice, too. Jews do not go out and try to persuade others to become Jewish. However, they welcome those who, because they are convinced it is right for them, decide to become Jews – although it is not easy for people to do this.

Abraham, who lived 3500 years ago, is usually thought of as the first Jew. In the Bible, the book of Genesis describes him as leaving his birthplace, Ur of the Chaldees in ancient Mesopotamia, and journeying to a new country, the land of Israel, given to him and his descendants. Although Abraham is spoken of as the first Jew, Judaism is a religion with roots that stretch even further back in history. From the religion of the ancient Israelites worshipping their local gods at hill-top altars, it had developed by 200CE (200 AD) into a system with rules covering every aspect of daily life.

As Jews do not recognise Jesus as the Messiah and therefore cannot say Before Christ (BC), which means 'Before the Messiah'; or Anno Domini (AD), which means 'In the Year of the Lord', dates in the calendar are shown with CE after them instead of AD.

Judaism calls for its followers to organise their lives in a certain way. There are commandments, *mitzvot*, to be followed, and a variety of things are forbidden. Jews are told to study the *Torah*, the five books of Moses from Genesis to Deuteronomy (in the Bible), which is the basis of Jewish teaching. According to the Bible, the Torah was given by God to Moses on Mount Sinai, in the Sinai Desert. So although Abraham was supposed to be the first Jew, it was not until the time of Moses that the Jews were told what God wanted from them. From then on, the law was developed so that there were rules for most things in everyday life, from what to eat to how to pray, how to study, and how to rest. Most Jews try to keep some, if not all, of these laws.

Beginnings

When Abraham left Ur, as the story goes, Mesopotamia
was already a great civilisation, with fine buildings,
a great literature, and beautiful jewellery. They also had
many temples, called *ziggurats*, which were built to look
like steps into the sky, because the Babylonians believed
that you could get nearer to the gods in that way. Many of
the early stories in the Torah are similar to Babylonian
myths – this is true of the story of the Tower of Babel,
which is probably about a ziggurat, as well as the story of
Noah, which is similar to the Babylonian story of
Gilgamesh – and there are many others.

Abraham and his tribe were probably nomads,
wandering over the pastures with their sheep and goats.
At some stage they made a great journey across the desert
into the land of Canaan on the coast of the Mediterranean.
From there, some generations later, Abraham's grandson
and his sons went to Egypt. Although there are a lot of
stories in the Bible about the Israelites in Egypt, there is
very little evidence of this in Egypt itself. But it does seem
likely that they went there and that they stayed there for
hundreds of years. Things became difficult when the
Egyptians started treating the Israelites as slaves.
According to the Bible, they wanted to leave, but as the
Egyptian king, the Pharoah, would not let them go, God
sent plagues to the Egyptians. After this, the Israelites left
in a great hurry, and crossed through the waters of the
Red Sea which miraculously parted for them. Much of
this may be only legend, but the story of the journey from
slavery to freedom is celebrated by Jews every year at the
festival of the Passover (*Pesach*).

Ancient Egyptian
frieze showing
captive Jews

It was Moses who led the Israelites out of Egypt. He was probably the greatest leader of the Jewish people, but, because once, in the wilderness, he committed the grave sin of disobeying God, he was not allowed into the Promised Land of Israel. Instead, he led the people on a journey through the wilderness which took forty years, but was only allowed to see the Promised Land from the top of a mountain before he died.

Some of the treasures found at Ur

The giving of the Law

While the Israelites were in the wilderness they were given the Torah – the Law. According to the Book of Exodus in the Bible, Moses went up Mount Sinai to collect the stone tablets of the Law from God. While he was gone, the Israelites became restless and difficult. They asked Aaron, Moses' brother, who was in charge, to make them another god to worship, since they were not convinced that God was looking after them. Aaron asked them all to give him their gold jewellery which they had brought with them from

Egypt. He melted it down and made a golden calf, and the Israelites then worshipped this gold idol. Moses was furious when he came down from the mountain, and in his rage he smashed the tablets. Moses made a second attempt, going up the mountain again, and this time after the Israelites had listened while Moses read out the law on the stone tablets, they replied "We will do it and we will obey." (Ex 19:8). These were the Ten Commandments, the basis of the Torah, the teaching recognised as the only authority in Judaism.

The Torah is made up of the five Books of Moses – the Books of Genesis, Exodus, Leviticus, Numbers, and Deuteronomy. It is read during synagogue service on the Sabbath morning every Saturday. It is studied and discussed by generation after generation of Jews from the humblest to the wisest. One of the most important commandments of Judaism is to study, and the most respected people of all in Jewish communities are teachers and scholars.

The scrolls of the Torah are written on parchment – a fine leather material – by a scribe who concentrates extremely hard on writing God's word. It is a difficult task to copy scrolls patiently, and great care has to be taken not to make mistakes.

Every week a new section of the scroll is read aloud in each synagogue. Each year the whole Torah is completed and started again, and Jews listen and study the law. Although modern scholars think that the Torah is the work of human beings – and all the evidence points that way – Orthodox Jews believe in the tradition that it is literally God's word, dictated to Moses.

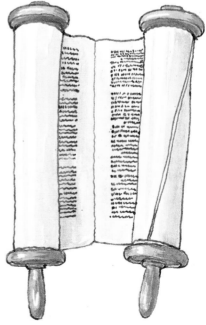

Torah scrolls

The Kings and the Exiles

The Israelites went into the Promised Land of Israel, led by Joshua, who was Moses' successor. They had to fight with the Canaanite tribes who already lived there, and there were many battles. Joshua's most famous victory was the Battle of Jericho, where the city walls fell down when his men blew trumpets. Joshua was succeeded by the judges, who led the people into further battles. Gradually, the Israelites defeated the Canaanite tribes and settled in towns like Shechem and, later on, Jerusalem.

Soon the Israelites were asking for a king like the other tribes around them. They complained to Samuel, the prophet, who unwillingly consulted God on the subject. Eventually, a man called Saul became king. He was a brave warrior, but a moody, violent and difficult man. The story is told that he tried to murder David, his son Jonathan's great friend, with a spear. Whatever the truth, David and Saul were rivals, and when Saul and Jonathan were both killed in battle, David became king and his royal line continued for hundreds of years.

With copper mining and international trade, David and his son Solomon built up the country into a great empire, and its influence reached far and wide. But, when Solomon died, things were already declining. The kingdom was then split between his son Rehoboam, and his rival, Jeroboam, who was a general. The northern

The Wailing Wall at Jerusalem

kingdom under Jeroboam only lasted a short, troubled time after this, and in 721BCE the Assyrians forced the ten northern tribes into permanent exile. The southern kingdom of Judah lasted another 135 years, until it was defeated and its people exiled by the Babylonians. The exile in Babylonia was a different experience from the Assyrian one, and when the Jews were given the chance to return, many preferred to remain. They had settled down well in their new country, and lived good lives there by following the prophet Jeremiah's instructions: "Seek the peace of the city to which you have been carried away captive . . . build houses . . . plant gardens . . . pray for its welfare . . ." It was in Babylonia, nearly a thousand years later, that the greatest legal work of Judaism was completed, the Babylonian Talmud.

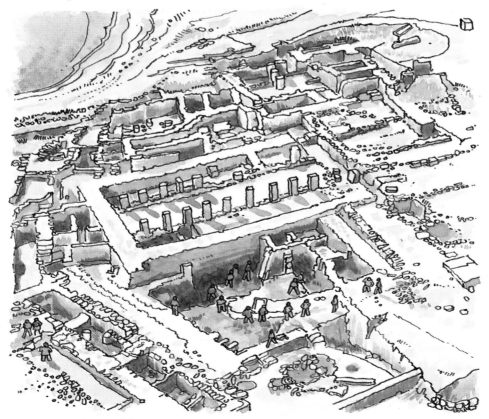

The Palace at Hazor

The Golden Age in Spain

Judaism flourished in Babylon and Palestine, and soon spread all over the known world. After the Romans destroyed the Second Temple in 70 CE, Jews travelled all over the Roman Empire, and in later centuries were found in France, Germany, Italy, North Africa, and Spain. Under Islamic rule in Spain there was a golden age of Jewish poetry and philosophy – Jewish learning blossomed in the southern Spanish cities of Granada, Cordoba and Seville. Much of the writing was done in Arabic, but it was later translated into Hebrew, and from Hebrew into Latin. It was often by this route that scientific knowledge, first discovered by the Greeks, travelled to the countries of northern Europe.

Studying the Talmud

The Jews of Spain and southern France in the Middle Ages were great scholars – they had often studied medicine and science, usually learnt from the Arab scientists of Spain and North Africa. There were also great poets – men such as Solomon ibn Gabirol and Judah Halevi. But as well as their great talents in other fields, their Jewish learning was of a very high standard. They studied the *Mishnah* and *Talmud*, the great works of Jewish law which formed the basis of all discussion on the law. The Mishnah was completed in about 200 CE, edited by a great rabbi, Judah Ha-nasi – which means Judah the Prince. Throughout southern France, Spain and North Africa, they developed schools for study of the Law, and in old Cairo, in Egypt, there flourished the greatest of the teachers and commentators, Moses Maimonides. He was born in Cordoba, in southern Spain, but his family fled because of persecution. He became a great doctor and statesman. But he was also the author of large numbers of commentaries, codes of law, philosophical works and answers to questions sent to him by Jewish communities all over the world. Despite much disapproval, he tried to condense Jewish belief into a kind of creed, now called the thirteen principles of the faith. After a brilliant life – of which he used every moment – he died in 1204.

Statue of Maimonides

Trouble in the Middle Ages

Although Jews flourished in Spain, those in other parts of
Europe had a varied reception. In many countries they
became the personal possession of the king. The system
by which Jews "belonged" to the ruler had drawbacks.
Sometimes this meant protection from persecution, but it
also meant being squeezed for money to pay for wars and
castles. Favours were easily withdrawn and Jews could
find themselves presented as a 'gift' to another ruler – to
settle a debt perhaps, or to be a dowry. One ruler would
expel them and another would refuse to admit them. And
they were seen as useful for only one purpose, money-
lending. Much of this was due to ignorance, but part of it
was the fault of the Christian Church, which, in 1215,
published a document containing some very harsh rules
for Jews, such as having to wear a special badge. Jews
were said to be responsible for all evils, and were killed
wholesale. When, for instance, the Black Death wiped out
a third of the population of Europe, the Jews were
accused of poisoning the wells. No evidence was required
– they were simply massacred. They fled from one
country to another in central Europe – from what is now
Germany to other areas, one of which is Poland today, to
start new centres of Jewish life.

The King of Castile decides to expel the Jews

All this was typical of a mood throughout Europe. Jews in England were accused of killing children to make unleavened bread for Passover, and of going into churches in secret to desecrate communion bread and wine, so that it would not be fit to use. The leaders of the first Crusade, in 1095, had suggested that the Jews, as killers of Christ – the false accusation that sometimes carries on to this very day – should be killed on the way to Jerusalem. One crusader, Peter the Hermit, led a campaign of destruction along the banks of the Rhine in 1096. He wanted to kill all the Jews in Germany. But the Crusades were supposed to be expeditions to take Jerusalem into Christian hands, and attack its Moslem rulers.

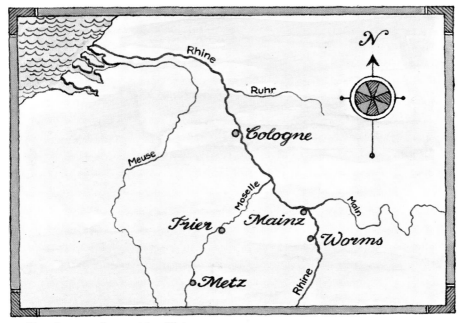

The destruction on the Rhine

It is a sad and terrible story, and it gets worse. England expelled its Jews in 1290. France did the same in 1394. And in Italy and Germany, Jews were made to live in ghettoes, closed parts of cities, where they lived in over-crowded conditions, that were very unhealthy even for those times.

Eastern Europe and Persecution

Through all these persecutions, Jewish life flourished where it could. Jews studied, wrote and prayed, and new communities in Eastern Europe grew up in an atmosphere of deep religious activity. Poland and Russia had communities of great learning. There were Jews all over North Africa, and in Holland, Italy, Germany and some parts of France. In Poland and Russia a great mystical tradition grew up. Saintly rabbis became leaders of the communities and teachers of simple people. They founded dynasties of teachers, and Jews flocked to hear their favourite *rebbe* or rabbi. Though much of this way of life was lost in the destruction of the Jews by the Nazis between 1939 and 1945, some people still follow this tradition in Israel and America. These people are called Chassidim, "the pious ones".

Despite many troubles at the beginning of the nineteenth century, the Jews of Europe began to emerge from the ghettoes. They studied other subjects as well as the Bible and the Talmud, and went to schools and universities. The world was opening up, and they too became more open-minded, prepared to dress like everyone else and, in some cases, to pray in German or English. A new, modern Judaism began – Reform Judaism – and it grew in Germany, Britain and America. Jews felt free for the first time in hundreds of years.

Shetl life

But they were not as safe as they thought. For in Russia violent attacks on Jews began in the reign of Tsar Nicholas I (1825–55) and carried on beyond the Russian revolution of 1917. The Kishinev massacre in 1904, when thousands of Jews were killed, shocked the world. Huge numbers of Jews fled from Russia to Germany, Austria, England and, especially, America.

But at the same time there was growing anti-Semitism in France, where an army captain called Dreyfus was unjustly accused of selling secrets to the enemy, and after a terrible, unjust trial was imprisoned in exile. He was innocent – and many people thought he was victimised because he was Jewish. This was partly true but there were other political reasons for his accusation, which divided the French people. Although there was a public outcry, it still took years to clear his name.

Captain Alfred Dreyfus

The anti-Semitism shown publicly in Europe and in Russia was only part of what existed under the surface. The greatest attack on Jews was still to come, by the Nazis in the Second World War from 1939 to 1945.

The Holocaust

The greatest catastrophe that has ever happened to the Jewish people was the Nazi persecution and extermination of six million Jewish men, women and children between 1939 and 1945. The Nazis killed other people too, particularly gypsies, mentally handicapped people, and Communists. But it was the Jews who were singled out for the greatest hatred and abuse. From 1933 onwards they had gradually been treated worse and worse in Germany and had become victims of a long campaign of violence. It affected German Jews of all kinds – rich and poor, the observant – those who practised their faith – and the non-observant – those who did not – young and old. Jewish children suffered at school, by being singled out as not being *Aryan* (of pure German blood as far back as grandparents), and old Jewish people were made to scrub the streets on their hands and knees.

Distressing though this persecution was, it bore no comparison with the terrible killing of Jews all over Europe after the Second World War had begun. Concentration camps where millions of Jews were imprisoned became extermination camps. In some, like Treblinka and Auschwitz, over a million people were murdered or starved to death. Other Jews, Communists, mentally handicapped people and other victims never got as far as a camp, but were merely rounded up and shot on the spot. The Jewish world has not really recovered from this experience even now. The mourning continues, and the attempt to find some meaning in the terrible things which took place. But one good thing happened afterwards, and though it was no comfort for what had happened it did give a little hope to the stunned Jewish community. This was the foundation of the State of Israel, in 1948.

From a drawing by a child in a Concentration camp

It did not come without fighting, and without the loss of land for other people. There have been wars about it since, such as the Six Day War in 1967 and the Yom Kippur War in 1973, and the fight still goes on today. In 1948, Britain handed over the Protectorate of Palestine to the Jews for them to establish the new nation of Israel. The people who already lived there, the Palestinians, claim a right to their land and this has led to many conflicts. Some Israelis claim that the land is theirs because, according to the Bible, God gave it to them. Others say that it was promised to them in 1917 under the Balfour Declaration, by the British who ruled Palestine at the time, and that the Jewish people have built it up. It is now a beautiful country and includes farming land rescued from what was once desert. It is also a great centre of Jewish learning.

18

The life-cycle

Jews have many customs as they go through their lives. Baby boys are circumcised on the eighth day after birth, when the foreskin is cut away from the penis. At 13, boys are *bar-mitzvah*, and in some synagogues, girls are *bat-mitzvah* (meaning 'daughter of the commandment') when they read from the Scroll of the Law, or Torah, in Hebrew, which almost all Jewish children learn at religion school. Boys are then said to become men, responsible for carrying out all the religious duties, *mitzvot*. This includes wearing a prayershawl *tallit*, being included in the ten men needed to conduct any full service, and being called as a witness.

Boy wearing a tallit

A wedding ring

In Reform and Liberal congregations, the two types of non-orthodox Judaism in Britain, boys and girls are not regarded as adults at 13, and although the ceremony takes place then, their religious education continues until 15 or 16, when in some synagogues there is a confirmation service.

Jewish weddings take place under a canopy, *chuppah*, with the couple and their parents, and the rabbi there. The couple share a cup of wine during the ceremony, and the bridegroom usually breaks a glass. No-one quite knows why, but it may be something to do with remembering suffering during times of joy. The wife is given the written marriage contract, *ketubbah*, at the end of the service. In ancient times, a bride's dowry was sometimes returned to her if she was divorced. In Jewish law, a woman cannot divorce her husband. A man can divorce his wife though, and there is no ruling against

A modern wedding

remarriage in a synagogue after divorce.

At the time of a death, Jews have a complicated but helpful mourning ritual, which is followed by many, but not all, members of the community. It is divided up into three parts. First the *shiva*, Hebrew for seven, the seven days of deep mourning after the funeral, when the principal mourners stay at home and are visited by friends and family. A service is held in the house each evening. After that comes *shloshim*, Hebrew for thirty, a period of lesser mourning for thirty days, and finally a further eleven months, where *kaddish*, the mourner's prayer, is said every day. As a system it corresponds well with the pattern of grief experienced by many bereaved people. In death, social differences disappear, and everyone has just a plain coffin and a simple shroud, however wealthy or poor they were.

The Sabbath

Food plays an important part in Jewish life. There are dietary laws which forbid the eating of animals except those that chew the cud and have a cloven (split) hoof. Only fish with fins and scales may be eaten so shellfish is forbidden, and there is a list of forbidden birds, mainly birds of prey. There is also a rule forbidding the mixing of milk and meat. Not all Jews follow these dietary laws, but orthodox Jews usually do. But dietary laws are only one part of it. Each festival has particular foods associated with it – unleavened bread, *matzah*, at Passover, cheese-cake and dairy foods at Pentecost, *Shavuot*, potato pancakes, at *Chanukkah* (the festival of dedication) and fruit of all kinds at Tabernacles, *Sukkot*.

The Sabbath begins on Friday at sundown, for all days run from sundown to sundown, and ends on Saturday evening. At the beginning of the Sabbath, the woman of the household lights two Sabbath candles. Some families go to synagogue before the Sabbath starts, to greet the Sabbath. In other families, only the men go, and in others, the whole family goes to synagogue after their meal – it depends what kind of synagogue they go to.

The main part of the Friday evening for most families is the Sabbath meal. Usually, the best food of the

A plaited Sabbath candle

week is eaten. The table is laid with a white cloth, everyone sits down together, and there is singing both before and after the meal. Before the meal begins there is *kiddush*, the blessings over the wine and bread which everyone shares. The bread, called *challah*, is beautifully plaited and there are two loaves, as a reminder that the children of Israel collected two portions of manna in the wilderness on Fridays. The Sabbath continues until Saturday night, with everyone going to synagogue on Saturday morning to hear the Torah being read. The

Sabbath finishes with a ceremony called *havdallah*, meaning 'division', when a plaited candle is put out by dousing it in wine, and everyone smells sweet spices, to symbolise the sweetness of the Sabbath, the day of rest.

Challah and kiddush cup

The Calendar

Unlike most other religions, Jews begin each new year with a solemn serious time. The Jewish calendar is a lunar one, which means it goes according to the phases of the moon. This way, a year has nearly thirteen months. However the Jewish Calendar counts only twelve of these, so to bring the seasons back into line with the solar calendar, an extra month, called *Adar Sheni*, the second Adar, has to be added occasionally. The New Year, *Rosh Hashanah*, is normally in late September – the first of the Hebrew month Tishri. It is a solemn day, for it is the start of ten days of penitence. But it is also a day of joy, as the start of a new year, and a day of memorial – looking back to remember the history of the Jewish people, as well as forwards into the New Year.

It often begins with a special family meal, with the New Year round loaf, to symbolise the roundness of the year. Apples are eaten too, dipped in honey, for a sweet year.

The service, solemn and sombre, is broken up by the blowing of the *shofar*, the ram's horn. The exact reason for this is not known – perhaps it was to attract God's attention, perhaps it was a sign of true repentance – but it is blown with a series of different, splendid calls – a thrilling sound.

New Year starts the ten days of Penitence, leading up to *Yom Kippur*, the Day of Atonement, the most solemn day of the year. It is a fast day. The synagogue overflows with people. Everyone, even the least observant, comes to ask for forgiveness. The service lasts all the following day. It is exhausting, and moving. At the end, people feel they have repented; have looked for forgiveness. The legend is

that on New Year God opens the book of life, and that in the ten days of penitence he decides who is to live and who to die. But according to one of the most important prayers of the day, "Repentance, prayer and charity avert the severity of the

The ram's horn (shofar)

decree." So in the ten days, and on *Yom Kippur* itself, people have the chance to change the judgment, to plead with God. And as they confess their sins, either privately or in a communal prayer, that is what they are trying to do.

Inside a synagogue

Festivals

The first action after the end of *Yom Kippur*, even before breaking the fast, is to start building the *sukkah* with a branch or two. The sukkah is the booth built for the duration of Sukkot, the festival of Tabernacles. It is partly open at the top – there are gaps so that one can see the sky. It is a very temporary building, but the custom is for Jews to live in it for the week of Sukkot, or, at the very least, to eat in it. In England, the climate often makes this difficult! It is built as a reminder of the simple temporary nature of the huts in which the Israelites lived in the wilderness. It also serves as a reminder of the temporary nature of life. Sukkot is the most important harvest festival of the year, when produce used to be taken to Jerusalem, to the Temple. Even now the sukkah is decorated with fruit and flowers, and in many synagogues all over the world fruit, vegetables and other kinds of food are brought in to be given to elderly and disabled people.

The palm (lulav) being waved, on Sukkot

Sukkot lasts for a week. The eighth day, or for orthodox Jews outside Israel, the ninth, is the festival of the rejoicing of the law, *Simchat Torah*, when the reading of the scroll is completed at Deuteronomy and begun again at Genesis. The scrolls are carried in procession around the synagogue, there is singing and dancing, children carry flags, and are given apples and sweets. The solemn atmosphere, which had lasted from New Year to the Day of Atonement, is completely dispelled in the joy of the people.

In November/December there is the minor festival of *Chanukkah*, which means dedication. During this festival, a candelabra (*menorah* or *chanukkiyah*) is lit – one candle on the first night, two on the second, and so on for eight days. The legend says that when the Maccabees had driven the Seleucid Greeks out of the Temple in Jerusalem, there was enough oil for the eternal light for only one day – but by a miracle it lasted for eight. Children are usually given presents on each of the eight days of Chanukkah and, in Christian countries, Chanukkah has acquired greater importance because of its closeness in the calendar to Christmas.

A Chanukkah menorah

Purim, Passover and Pentecost

In the early spring, around March, comes the festival of *Purim*, which means the drawing of lots. It is based on the book of Esther in the Bible. When Haman, courtier to King Ahasuerus, wanted to destroy the Jews he was foiled by Queen Esther and her uncle Mordecai, and Haman was killed instead. The story is read aloud, there is booing and stamping when Haman's name is mentioned, and cheers for Esther and Mordecai. Special cakes are made – *Hamantaschen* – which means Haman's ears – and an atmosphere of carnival prevails, with fancy-dress and plays about the story of Purim.

Later in the spring comes Passover, *Pesach*, which celebrates the freeing of the Israelites from slavery in Egypt. A service is held around the table, called a *seder*, reading from a special prayer book called a *haggadah*. Various special foods are eaten, such as parsley dipped in salt water, to symbolise the tears shed by the Israelites as slaves, and horseradish, to symbolize the bitterness of

A Passover plate

A Purim play

their sufferings. For the whole week of Passover, Jews eat no leaven, nothing with yeast in it, and nothing which expands when it is cooked. Instead they eat a special flat 'unleavened' bread called *matzah*. Other important symbols during the Passover service are the leg bone of a lamb, a reminder of the Paschal lamb whose blood was daubed on the gateposts of the Israelite houses, so the angel of death would pass by. The Cup of Elijah placed on the *seder* table, filled but never drunk from, is symbolic of the Messiah, and of waiting for the unexpected guest.

Seven weeks after Passover, which is the first of the harvest festivals for the new born lambs and the early grain crop, comes Pentecost, called *Shavuot*, the feast of weeks. It is both a dairy festival – the middle harvest festival concentrating on dairy foods and fruits – and a historical one, for it records the giving of the Torah on Mount Sinai. It is celebrated by many Jews by staying up all night and studying and reading from the Torah. Many modern Jews also have their confirmation service, for 16 year olds, on Shavuot. The synagogue is especially decorated with flowers, and fruit is eaten in as many different varieties as possible.

Modern Jews

Jews live all over the world. The once important and large communities of Germany, Poland and Hungary are small now; in many places where there used to be thriving synagogues there are only one or two Jews. But there are other new communities elsewhere. Israel is, of course, the most important example – but it is not the only one. There are growing communities in Australia, in some parts of the United States, and in France. There are also many Jews in the Soviet Union, although it is hard to find out exact numbers, and many face persecution: any religious observances are frowned on and Jewish books are hard to obtain. Despite difficulties, Jews continue to live around the world.

There are many different kinds of Jews. Some do not practise the faith at all but claim they are Jewish simply by loyalty to other Jews and a shared history. Others are extremely observant, from the *Chassidim* to be found in the USA, Israel and England, to the other varieties of extreme orthodoxy, and the Sephardic (Spanish, Portuguese and North African) Jews from the Yemen and North Africa, now living in Israel. The Chassidim are very pious Jews, recognisable by their distinctive clothes. They were originally all followers of an eighteenth century rabbi called the Baal Shem Tov, the master of the good name.

Most Jews are not recognisable by their clothes or their features. Jewish houses can usually be recognised by the *mezuzah*, a small box on the door-frame containing some verses from the Torah, but often this is not immediately visible. Jews of all colours are to be found; black from Ethiopia, the *Falashas* – brown from India, Iraq and Iran, and all shades of white. A twelfth century Jewish traveller, Benjamin of Tudela, was surprised to discover that Jews in Mongolia looked just like other Mongolians!

Most Jews look the same as the people amongst whom they live, and are part of a people with a shared history and religion. They are not a race with special characteristics. Wherever they live, individuals may flourish or do badly, just like everyone else. But they form their own religious communities and build synagogues, schools and cemeteries for their own use.

The Jews Today

Despite a world population of some thirteen or fourteen
million people, now fewer than before the Holocaust,
Judaism is thriving with new vitality. Israel has provided
a new centre, with much Jewish learning coming from it,
and the love of many *diaspora* Jews – those living outside
Israel – turned to it. The USA actually has a larger Jewish
population than Israel, and some areas have a strong
Jewish 'flavour' such as Brooklyn in New York, and parts
of Philadelphia and Cincinnatti. Jewish books are
published, Jewish universities, schools and training
colleges for rabbis thrive, and Jewish newspapers
circulate widely. Most important of all, Jews mix freely in
American society. The same is true in Britain, with its

much smaller Jewish population. But there is still some
anti-Semitism, varying in strength from one country to
another. Jews in France have perhaps suffered worst in
Europe, inculding a quite recent bombing in a Paris
synagogue. Jews are thoroughly mixed into British and
American society. There are Jewish actors, politicians
(at the time of writing, four British Cabinet members are
Jewish), teachers, lecturers, market traders. Sammy Davis
Junior is Jewish; so are Helen Shapiro and Woody Allen.
And there are many more. Some were born Jewish, others
became Jewish, either because they were convinced it
was right or because of wanting the same faith as that of
their marriage partner.

A feeling of shock remains about all the people killed
by the Nazis – and it will take many years before most
Jews, and many others, can understand how it could
happen. Jews also watch over Israel with the sort of love
parents have for children, critical of every wrong move
and praising it for everything good. Many see it as the
one good thing which has come out of the holocaust; a
land to which all Jews may go.

But in ordinary everyday terms, Jews live ordinary
lives, well accepted by those amongst whom they live.
They hope to carry on their religion with love and
devotion, teaching the values of the Torah and the
prophets to their children, and they to theirs, in peace.
That is not always possible, but it is their constant hope.

Jewish Terms

Barmitzvah – a coming of age ceremony for a boy when he reaches the age of 13

Bat-mitzvah – similar to the bar-mitzvah ceremony for boys, in Reform and Liberal synagogues, where men and women are equal in status

B.C.E. – Before the Common Era: equivalent to 'BC' in a date.

C.E. – Common Era: equivalent to 'AD' in a date; eg. 1986 AD.

Challah – plaited bread-loaves for the Sabbath meal.

Chanukkah – the festival of dedication, 25th Kislev for eight days

Chanukkiyah – the Chanukkah menorah

Charoset – paste made of apples, nuts, honey, cinnamon and wine eaten at Passover to symbolise the mortar used by the Israelites when they were slaves to Pharoah in Egypt

Chassidim – pious Jews, usually followers of a particular rabbi. It was a sect started by followers of a rabbi called Baal Shem Tov, in the eighteenth century

Chuppah – wedding canopy

Diaspora – term used for Jews living outside the land of Israel

Haggadah – prayerbook for Passover

Hamantaschen – Haman's ears. Cakes made for Purim, stuffed with poppy seeds, eaten to celebrate Haman's defeat

Havdallah – ceremony for the end of the Sabbath

Kaddish – the mourner's prayer

Ketubah – marriage contract (document)

Kiddush – blessings over wine on Sabbath days and festivals

Liberal Judaism – in Britain, one of the two progressive movements in Judaism. It does not believe in the divine authority of Jewish law, and it attempts to practise Judaism in accord with moden life

Lulav – palm branch with willow and myrtle, held in the hands together with an etrog (citron), and waved at the festival of Sukkot

Matzah – unleavened bread

Menorah – 7 branched candlestick used in the Temple. But there is also the Chanukkah menorah (chanukkiyah) which is used during that festival

Mezuzah – box on the door-frame of Jewish house containing verses from Deuteronomy

Mishnah – code of Jewish law, probably edited by Judah-ha-Nasi in about 200 C.E.

Mitzvot – religious duties, from the word for commandments.

Nazi – member of the National Socialist party of Germany; the Nazi government under Hitler ruled Germany from 1933–45

Orthodox Judaism – Judaism observed totally in accordance with the law. The main belief is that the Torah was given by God to Moses on Mount Sinai, and that the whole Torah is God's word.

Passover – Pesach. The festival commemorating the Exodus running for seven days from 14th of Nisan

Purim – the festival of lots. 13th–14th Adar. A great carnival

Rabbi – teacher and leader of the community

Reform Judaism – one of the two progressive movements in Britain. It does not believe in the divine authority of all Jewish law, but can be quite traditional in practice. In the USA, Reform is the most liberal wing in Judaism

Rosh Hashanah – Jewish New Year (2nd for Orthodox Jews) *Tishri*. The beginning of the ten days of repentance

Seder – Passover table-meal and service

Shabbat – Friday evening to Saturday evening each week. The day of rest called the Sabbath

Shavuot – Pentecost, the festival of the giving of the law, fifty days after Passover on *Sivan* 6th

Shiva – seven days of mourning

Shloshim – thirty days of lesser mourning

Simchat Torah – festival of the rejoicing of the law

Sukkah – booth made of branches, open to the sky, built to live in during Sukkot

Sukkot – Tabernacles, 15th *Tishri*. The third (and main) harvest festival. Jews build booths to commemorate their temporary buildings in the desert

Tallit – prayershawl with fringes

Talmud – discussion of Jewish law based on the Mishnah with much additional material. One Talmud was produced in Babylonia, the other in Palestine. It was probably completed in about 500 C.E.

Torah – Five Books of Moses, sometimes called the Pentateuch. Genesis, Exodus, Leviticus, Numbers and Deuteronomy

Yom Kippur – Day of Atonement, observed on 10th *Tishri*. A fast day on which Jews repent of their sins.